INSIDE THE MIND OF BILL GATES

SHAUN GREEN

Copyright © 2014 Shaun Green

All rights reserved.

ISBN: 1514162733
ISBN-13: 978-1514162736

CONTENTS

1	Introduction	1
2	About Business	3
3	About Himself and Family	7
4	About Microsoft	15
5	About Success	19
6	Quotes on a Variety of Topics	23
7	On Politics	37
8	On Technology	43
9	Philanthropy	55
10	Philosophy	59

ACKNOWLEDGMENTS

All quotes within this book are in the words of Bill Gates. Although every effort has been taken to ensure the accuracy of all text, the author apologises in the event of any mistakes.

1 INTRODUCTION

Bill Gates is the first and best known self-made billionaire within the software industry. Since his conception of Microsoft in the 1970s, he has continued his success with constant innovation to keep himself at the forefront of technological innovation.

Yet there is more to Gates than his entrepreneurship. Though he is still exceptionally wealthy, he is now known as much for his philanthropy as for his business skills. Indeed, had it not been for the massive amounts he has donated to charities across the world, he would be the richest man on the planet.

Bill Gates has always shown genuine concern for problems across the world and continues to help those most in need, earning him the respect of many throughout the world.

As you would expect from such a unique character, Gates has been quoted many times in the media on a wide variety of issues. This book brings you some of his most notable thoughts on everything from business to his personal life.

2 ABOUT BUSINESS

"Information technology and business are becoming inextricably interwoven. I don't think anybody can talk meaningfully about one without the talking about the other."

*

"Of my mental cycles, I devote maybe ten percent to business thinking. Business isn't that complicated. I wouldn't want to put it on my business card."

*

"In this business, by the time you realize you're in trouble, it's too late to save yourself. Unless you're running scared all the time, you're gone."

*

"Software innovation, like almost every other kind of innovation, requires the ability to collaborate and share ideas with other people, and to sit down and talk with customers and get their feedback and understand their needs."

*

"If you've found some way to educate yourself about engineering, stocks, or whatever it is, good employers will have some type of exam or interview and see a sample of your work."

*

"Apple has always leveraged technologies that the PC industry has driven to critical mass - the bus structures, the graphics cards, the peripherals, the connection networks, things like that - so they're kind of in the PC ecosystem and kind of not."

*

"Intellectual property has the shelf life of a banana."

*

"Steve Jobs' ability to focus in on a few things that count, get people who get user interface right, and market things as revolutionary are amazing things."

*

"Google's done a super good job on search; Apple's done a great job on the IPod."

*

"This is a fantastic time to be entering the business world, because business is going to change more in the next 10 years than it has in the last 50."

*

"Your most unhappy customers are your greatest source of learning."

*

"I'm an investor in a number of biotech companies, partly because of my incredible enthusiasm for the great innovations they will bring."

*

"The typical project design time for a large company like IBM - and they keep track of this - is a little over four years."

*

"In business, the idea of measuring what you are doing, picking the measurements that count like customer satisfaction and performance... you thrive on that."

*

"I believe in innovation and that the way you get innovation is you fund research and you learn the basic facts."

*

"China has many successful entrepreneurs and business people. I hope that more people of insight will put their talents to work to improve the lives of poor people in China and around the world, and seek solutions for them."

3 ABOUT HIMSELF AND FAMILY

"The 'Billionaire' song is what my kids tease me with. They sing it to me. It's funny."

*

"Whether I'm at the office, at home, or on the road, I always have a stack of books I'm looking forward to reading."

*

"I went to a public school through sixth grade, and being good at tests wasn't cool."

*

"Contrary to popular belief, I don't spend a whole lot of time following soccer. But as I have traveled around the world to better understand global development and health, I've learned that soccer is truly universal. No matter where I go, that's what kids are playing. That's what people are talking about."

*

"Well, I don't think there's any need for people to focus on my career."

*

"The only thing I understand deeply, because in my teens I was thinking about it, and every year of my life, is software. So I'll never be hands-on on anything except software."

*

"In ninth grade, I came up with a new form of rebellion. I hadn't been getting good grades, but I decided to get all A's without taking a book home. I didn't go to math class, because I knew enough and had read ahead, and I placed within the top 10 people in the nation on an aptitude exam."

*

"If I'd had some set idea of a finish line, don't you think I would have crossed it years ago?"

*

"My mom was on the United Way group that decides how to allocate the money and looks at all the different charities and makes the very hard decisions about where that pool of funds is going to go."

*

"Paper is no longer a big part of my day. I get 90% of my news online, and when I go to a meeting and want to jot things down, I bring my Tablet PC. It's fully synchronized with my office machine, so I have all the files I need. It also has a note-taking piece of software called OneNote, so all my notes are in digital form."

*

"My son likes to go see mines and electric plants, or the Large Hadron Collider, and we've had a chance to see a lot of interesting stuff."

*

"Certainly I'll never be able to put myself in the situation that people growing up in the less developed countries are in. I've gotten a bit of a sense of it by being out there and meeting people and talking with them."

*

"I'm a geek."

*

"Like almost everyone who uses e-mail, I receive a ton of spam every day. Much of it offers to help me get out of debt or get rich quick. It would be funny if it weren't so exciting."

*

"Understanding science and pushing the boundaries of science is what makes me immensely satisfied."

*

"I really had a lot of dreams when I was a kid, and I think a great deal of that grew out of the fact that I had a chance to read a lot."

*

"I'm not big on to-do lists. Instead, I use e-mail and desktop folders and my online calendar. So when I walk up to my desk, I can focus on the e-mails I've flagged and check the folders that are monitoring particular projects and particular blogs."

*

"I'm certainly well taken care of in terms of food and clothes."

*

"I have a particular relationship with Vinod Khosla because he's got a lot of very interesting science-based energy startups."

*

"If you're a person struggling to eat and stay healthy, you might have heard about Michael Jordan or Muhammad Ali, but you'll never have heard of Bill Gates."

*

"Money has no utility to me beyond a certain point."

*

"Me and my dad are the biggest promoters of an estate tax in the US. It's not a popular position."

*

"My wife thinks she's better than me at puzzles. I haven't given in on that one yet."

*

"OK, I have a nickname. My family calls me 'Trey' because I'm William the third. My dad has the same name, which is always confusing because my dad is well known, and I'm also known."

*

"I have an excellent memory, a most excellent memory."

*

"Legacy is a stupid thing! I don't want a legacy."

*

"I read a lot of obscure books and it is nice to open a book."

*

"I have a nice office. I have a nice house... So I'm not denying myself some great things. I just don't happen to have expensive hobbies."

*

"People are always coming up to me and saying, 'I heard your dad's speech, and it's really great.' And they'll mention some place I didn't even know my dad was going to."

4 ABOUT MICROSOFT

"Microsoft is not about greed. It's about innovation and fairness."

*

"Any version of Windows is going to have lots of great new things that people use and things that are tough."

*

"Certainly, the Windows share of servers is strong."

*

"The potential financial reward for building the 'next Windows' is so great that there will never be a shortage of new technologies seeking to challenge it."

*

"With Windows 8, Microsoft is trying to gain market share in what has been dominated by the iPad-type device. But a lot of those users are frustrated. They can't type. They can't create documents."

*

"Driving up the value of the advertising is a big commitment for Microsoft."

*

"People everywhere love Windows."

*

"Whether it's Google or Apple or free software, we've got some fantastic competitors and it keeps us on our toes."

*

"The thing about HD-DVD that is attractive to Microsoft is that it's very pro-consumer in letting you copy all movies up onto the hard disk."

*

"One thing I've always loved about the culture at Microsoft is there is nobody who is tougher on us, in terms of what we need to learn and do better, than the people in the company itself. You can walk down these halls, and they'll tell you, 'We need to do usability better, push this or that frontier.'"

*

"The outside perception and inside perception of Microsoft are so different. The view of Microsoft inside Microsoft is always kind of an underdog thing."

*

"I was lucky to be involved and get to contribute to something that was important, which is empowering people with software."

*

"Microsoft Research has a thing called the Sense Cam that, as you walk around, it's taking photos all the time. And the software will filter and find the ones that are interesting without having to think, 'Let's get out the camera and get that shot.' You just have that, and software helps you pick what you want."

*

"I have a company that is not Microsoft, called Corbis. Corbis is the operation that merged with Bettman Archives. It has nothing to do with Microsoft. It was intentionally done outside of Microsoft because Microsoft isn't interested."

*

"Outlook 2003 did create the idea of search folders and the whole Longhorn philosophy. You can see it at work in search folders, where instead of having to drop things into individual folders, and things exist only in one folder, you create these search folders and you have the criteria for the search folder."

*

"At Microsoft there are lots of brilliant ideas but the image is that they all come from the top - I'm afraid that's not quite right."

5 ABOUT SUCCESS

"The way to be successful in the software world is to come up with breakthrough software, and so whether it's Microsoft Office or Windows, its pushing that forward. New ideas, surprising the marketplace, so good engineering and good business are one in the same."

*

"I believe the returns on investment in the poor are just as exciting as successes achieved in the business arena, and they are even more meaningful!"

*

"I would counsel people to go to college, because it's one of the best times in your life in terms of who you meet and develop a broad set of intellectual skills."

*

"Success is a lousy teacher. It seduces smart people into thinking they can't lose."

*

"It's fine to celebrate success but it is more important to heed the lessons of failure."

*

"Some people, through luck and skill, end up with a lot of assets. If you're good at kicking a ball, writing software, investing in stocks, it pays extremely well."

*

"Well I think any author or musician is anxious to have legitimate sales of their products, partly so they're rewarded for their success, partly so they can go on and do new things."

*

"Everyone needs a coach. It doesn't matter whether you're a basketball player, a tennis player, a gymnast or a bridge player."

*

"In the long run, your human capital is your main base of competition. Your leading indicator of where you're going to be 20 years from now is how well you're doing in your education system."

*

"I can understand wanting to have millions of dollars; there's a certain freedom, meaningful freedom, that comes with that."

6 QUOTES ON A VARIETY OF TOPICS

"There are more people dying of malaria than any specific cancer."

*

"What's amazing is, if young people understood how doing well in school makes the rest of their life so much interesting, they would be more motivated. It's so far away in time that they can't appreciate what it means for their whole life."

*

"I have seen firsthand that agricultural science has enormous potential to increase the yields of small farmers and lift them out of hunger and poverty."

*

"Unfortunately, the highly curious student is a small percentage of the kids."

*

"In K-12, almost everybody goes to local schools. Universities are a bit different because kids actually do pick the university. The bizarre thing, though, is that the merit of university is actually how good the students going in are: the SAT scores of the kids going in."

*

"Measles will always show you if someone isn't doing a good job on vaccinations. Kids will start dying of measles."

*

"Nuclear energy, in terms of an overall safety record, is better than other energy."

*

"In energy, you have to plan and do research way in

advance, sometimes decades in advance to get a new system that's safer, doesn't require us to go around the world to get all our oil."

*

"If all my bridge coach ever told me was that I was 'satisfactory,' I would have no hope of ever getting better. How would I know who was the best? How would I know what I was doing differently?"

*

"It's the poorer people in tropical zones who will get really hit by climate change - as well as some ecosystems, which nobody wants to see disappear."

*

"In poor countries, we still need better ways to measure the effectiveness of the many government workers providing health services. They are the crucial link bringing tools such as vaccines and education to the people who need them most. How well trained are they? Are they showing up to work?"

*

"Unemployment rates among Americans who never went

to college are about double that of those who have a postsecondary education."

*

"Nigeria has moved into low-middle-income, but their north is very poor, and the health care systems there have broken down."

*

"The main thing that's missing in energy is an incentive to create things that are zero-CO_2-emitting and that have the right scale and reliability characteristics."

*

"Well, no one gives aid to Zimbabwe through the Mugabe government."

*

"The Center for Disease Control started out as the malaria war control board based in Atlanta. Partly because the head of Coke had some people out to his plantation, and they got infected with malaria, and partly 'cause all the military recruits were coming down and having a higher fatality rate from malaria while training than in the field."

*

"By the time we see that climate change is really bad, your ability to fix it is extremely limited... The carbon gets up there, but the heating effect is delayed. And then the effect of that heat on the species and ecosystem is delayed. That means that even when you turn virtuous, things are actually going to get worse for quite a while."

*

"The malaria parasite has been killing children and sapping the strength of whole populations for tens of thousands of years. It is impossible to calculate the harm malaria has done to the world."

*

"In American math classes, we teach a lot of concepts poorly over many years. In the Asian systems they teach you very few concepts very well over a few years."

*

"The ideal thing would be to have a 100 percent effective AIDS vaccine. And to have broad usage of that vaccine. That would literally break the epidemic."

*

"Until we're educating every kid in a fantastic way, until every inner city is cleaned up, there is no shortage of things to do."

*

"The trouble with energy farming is that the energy isn't always where you want to use it, and it isn't always when you want to use it."

*

"Innovations that are guided by smallholder farmers, adapted to local circumstances, and sustainable for the economy and environment will be necessary to ensure food security in the future."

*

"Considering their impact, you might expect mosquitoes to get more attention than they do. Sharks kill fewer than a dozen people every year, and in the U.S. they get a week dedicated to them on TV every year."

*

"If you're low-income in the United States, you have a higher chance of going to jail than you do of getting a four-year degree. And that doesn't seem entirely fair."

*

"Teaching's hard! You need different skills: positive reinforcement, keeping students from getting bored, commanding their attention in a certain way."

*

"The most interesting biofuel efforts avoid using land that's expensive and has high opportunity costs. They do this by getting onto other types of land, or taking advantage of byproducts that aren't used in the food chain today, or by intercropping."

*

"Living on $6 a day means you have a refrigerator, a TV, a cell phone, your children can go to school. That's not possible on $1 a day."

*

"Middle-income countries are the biggest users of GMOs. Places like Brazil."

*

"The world at large is less inequitable today than at any time in history. Number of people in abject poverty, as a percentage, is at all-time low."

*

"Today, we're very dependent on cheap energy. We just take it for granted - all the things you have in the house, the way industry works."

*

"Globalization has made copper and other minerals more valuable, and Ghana and Kenya have recently discovered mineral resources."

*

"Polio's pretty special because once you get an eradication, you no longer have to spend money on it; it's just there as a gift for the rest of time."

*

"What destroys more self-confidence than any other

educational thing in America is being assigned to some remedial math when you get into some college, and then it's not taught very well and you end up with this sense of, 'Hey, I can't really figure those things out.'"

*

"I don't think there's a... boundary between digital media and print media. Every magazine is doing an online version."

*

"We all know that there are these exemplars who can take the toughest students, and they'll teach them two-and-a-half years of math in a single year."

*

"If African farmers can use improved seeds and better practices to grow more crops and get them to market, then millions of families can earn themselves a better living and a better life."

*

"640K ought to be enough for anybody."

*

"If you're using first-class land for biofuels, then you're competing with the growing of food. And so you're actually spiking food prices by moving energy production into agriculture."

*

"In terms of mathematics textbooks, why can't you have the scale of a national market? Right now, we have a Texas textbook that's different from a California textbook that's different from a Massachusetts textbook. That's very expensive."

*

"Headlines, in a way, are what mislead you because bad news is a headline, and gradual improvement is not."

*

"Corruption is one of the most common reasons I hear in views that criticize aid."

*

"We all sort of do want incentives for creative people to

still exist at a certain level. You know, maybe rock stars shouldn't make as much; who knows? But you want as much creativity to take place in the future as took place in the past."

*

"Should there be cameras everywhere in outdoor streets? My personal view is having cameras in inner cities is a very good thing. In the case of London, petty crime has gone down. They catch terrorists because of it. And if something really bad happens, most of the time you can figure out who did it."

*

"Helping convene global stakeholders to establish a set of measurable, actionable and consensus-built goals focused on extreme poverty is invaluable."

*

"By 2018, an estimated 63 percent of all new U.S. jobs will require workers with an education beyond high school. For our young people to get those jobs, they first need to graduate from high school ready to start a postsecondary education."

*

"In 80% of the world, energy will be bought where it is economic. You have to help the rest of the world get energy at a reasonable price."

*

"According to Ethiopian custom, parents wait to name a baby because children often die in the first weeks of life."

*

"Now, we put out a lot of carbon dioxide every year, over 26 billion tons. For each American, it's about 20 tons. For people in poor countries, it's less than one ton. It's an average of about five tons for everyone on the planet. And, somehow, we have to make changes that will bring that down to zero."

*

"Climate change is a terrible problem, and it absolutely needs to be solved. It deserves to be a huge priority."

*

"India is more of an aid recipient than a provider of aid."

*

"The world has been very careful to pick very few diseases for eradication, because it is very tough."

*

"I think when smallpox was eliminated, the whole world got pretty excited about that because it's just such a dramatic success."

7 ON POLITICS

"The next time someone tells you we can trim the budget by cutting aid, I hope you will ask whether it will come at the cost of more people dying."

*

"If people want capital gains taxed more like the highest rate on income, that's a good discussion. Maybe that's the way to help close the deficit."

*

"Capitalism has shortfalls. It doesn't necessarily take care of the poor, and it underfunds innovation, so we have to offset that."

*

"One of the statistics that always amazes me is the approval of the Chinese government, not elected, is over 80 percent. The approval of the U.S. government, fully elected, is 19 percent. Well, we elected these people and they didn't elect those people. Isn't it supposed to be different? Aren't we supposed to like the people that we elected?"

*

"The U.S. couldn't even get rid of Saddam Hussein. And we all know that the EU is just a passing fad. They'll be killing each other again in less than a year. I'm sick to death of all these fascist lawsuits."

*

"As we look ahead into the next century, leaders will be those who empower others."

*

"You know capitalism is this wonderful thing that motivates people, it causes wonderful inventions to be done. But in this area of diseases of the world at large, it's really let us down."

*

"A lot of the things that will really improve the world fortunately aren't dependent on Washington doing something different."

*

"Well the protester I think is a very powerful thing. It's basically a mechanism of democracy that, along with capitalism, scientific innovation, those things have built the modern world. And it's wonderful that the new tools have empowered that protester so that state secrets, bad developments are not hidden anymore."

*

"I'm sorry that we have to have a Washington presence. We thrived during our first 16 years without any of this. I never made a political visit to Washington and we had no people here. It wasn't on our radar screen. We were just making great software."

*

"The U.S. immigration laws are bad - really, really bad. I'd say treatment of immigrants is one of the greatest injustices done in our government's name."

*

"Capitalism has worked very well. Anyone who wants to move to North Korea is welcome."

*

"Antitrust is the way that the government promotes markets when there are market failures. It has nothing to do with the idea of free information."

*

"Governments will always play a huge part in solving big problems. They set public policy and are uniquely able to provide the resources to make sure solutions reach everyone who needs them. They also fund basic research, which is a crucial component of the innovation that improves life for everyone."

*

"If you go back to 1800, everybody was poor. I mean everybody. The Industrial Revolution kicked in, and a lot of countries benefited, but by no means everyone."

*

"In a budget, how important is art versus music versus athletics versus computer programming? At the end of the day, some of those trade-offs will be made politically."

*

"I think the positive competition between states in India is one of the most positive dynamics that the country has."

*

"There are people who don't like capitalism, and people who don't like PCs. But there's no-one who likes the PC who doesn't like Microsoft."

*

"When a country has the skill and self-confidence to take action against its biggest problems, it makes outsiders eager to be a part of it."

*

"It's OK for China to invent cancer drugs that cure patients in the United States. We want them to catch up. But as the leader, we want to keep setting a very, very high standard. We don't want them to catch up because we're slowing down or, even worse, going into reverse."

8 ON TECHNOLOGY

"When you want to do your homework, fill out your tax return, or see all the choices for a trip you want to take, you need a full-size screen."

*

"If GM had kept up with technology like the computer industry has, we would all be driving $25 cars that got 1,000 MPG."

*

"Over time, yes, countries will need to look at specific GMO products like they look at drugs today, where they don't approve them all. They look hard at the safety and the testing. And they make sure that the benefits far outweigh any of the downsides."

*

"It's really kind of cool to have solar panels on your roof."

*

"On my desk I have three screens, synchronized to form a single desktop. I can drag items from one screen to the next. Once you have that large display area, you'll never go back, because it has a direct impact on productivity."

*

"Historically, privacy was almost implicit, because it was hard to find and gather information. But in the digital world, whether it's digital cameras or satellites or just what you click on, we need to have more explicit rules - not just for governments but for private companies."

*

"Certainly there's a phenomenon around open source. You know free software will be a vibrant area. There will be a lot of neat things that get done there."

*

"I've always been amazed by Da Vinci, because he worked out science on his own. He would work by drawing things and writing down his ideas. Of course, he designed all sorts of flying machines way before you could actually build something like that."

*

"For a highly motivated learner, it's not like knowledge is secret and somehow the Internet made it not secret. It just made knowledge easy to find. If you're a motivated enough learner, books are pretty good."

*

"Technology is just a tool. In terms of getting the kids working together and motivating them, the teacher is the most important."

*

"The nuclear approach I'm involved in is called a traveling-wave reactor, which uses waste uranium for fuel. There's a lot of things that have to go right for that dream to come true - many decades of building demo plants, proving the economics are right. But if it does, you could have cheaper energy with no CO_2 emissions."

*

"Security is, I would say, our top priority because for all the exciting things you will be able to do with computers - organizing your lives, staying in touch with people, being creative - if we don't solve these security problems, then people will hold back."

*

"Digital technology has several features that can make it much easier for teachers to pay special attention to all their students."

*

"This social-networking thing takes you to crazy places."

*

"It is hard to overstate how valuable it is to have all the incredible tools that are used for human disease to study plants."

*

"To create a new standard, it takes something that's not just a little bit different; it takes something that's really new and really captures people's imagination, and the Macintosh, of all the machines I've ever seen, is the only one that meets that standard."

*

"Digital reading will completely take over. It's lightweight and it's fantastic for sharing. Over time it will take over."

*

"I think the thing we see is that as people are using video games more, they tend to watch passive TV a bit less. And so using the PC for the Internet, playing video games, is starting to cut into the rather unbelievable amount of time people spend watching TV."

*

"In the old generation, if one kid bought a PlayStation 2 and the other kid bought an Xbox, at his house you played PlayStation, at your house you played Xbox. Now that it's online, all those early buyers who... you want to play with, they've got their reputation online of who they are and how good they are at these games."

*

"Harnessing steam power required many innovations, as William Rosen chronicles in the book 'The Most Powerful Idea in the World.'"

*

"It's a nice reader, but there's nothing on the iPad I look at and say, 'Oh, I wish Microsoft had done it.'"

*

"It's easier to add things on to a PC than it's ever been before. It's one click, and boom, it comes down."

*

"People want to watch whatever video they want to watch whenever they want to watch. If you provision your Internet infrastructure adequately, you can do that."

*

"The advance of technology is based on making it fit in so that you don't really even notice it, so it's part of everyday life."

*

"The difference between a stranger sending you a message that you might be interested in at a very low volume level, no repetition, just sending it to very few people, and that being done as spam - those things get close enough that you want to be careful never to filter out something that's legitimate."

*

"Music, even with these dial-up connections you have to the Internet, is very practical to download."

*

"3D is a way of organizing things, particularly as we're getting much more media information on the computer, a lot more choices, a lot more navigation than we've ever had before."

*

"Since when has the world of computer software design been about what people want? This is a simple question of evolution. The day is quickly coming when every knee will bow down to a silicon fist, and you will all beg your binary gods for mercy."

*

"Given how few young people actually read the newspaper, it's a good thing they'll be reading a newspaper on a screen."

*

"Eventually you won't think of 'the Internet business.' You'll think of it more like news, weather, sports, but even that taxonomy isn't clear."

*

"Innovation is moving at a scarily fast pace."

*

"I think it's fair to say that personal computers have become the most empowering tool we've ever created. They're tools of communication, they're tools of creativity, and they can be shaped by their user."

*

"The first rule of any technology used in a business is that automation applied to an efficient operation will magnify the efficiency. The second is that automation applied to an inefficient operation will magnify the inefficiency."

*

"Oh, I think there are a lot of people who would be buying and selling online today that go up there and they get the information, but then when it comes time to type in their credit card they think twice because they're not sure about how that might get out and what that might mean for them."

*

"Software substitution, whether it's for drivers or waiters or nurses - it's progressing. Technology over time will reduce demand for jobs, particularly at the lower end of skill set."

*

"A lot of people assume that creating software is purely a solitary activity where you sit in an office with the door closed all day and write lots of code."

*

"Software is a great combination between artistry and engineering."

*

"Internet TV and the move to the digital approach is quite revolutionary. TV has historically has been a broadcast medium with everybody picking from a very finite number of channels."

*

"In order for the United States to do the right things for the long term, it appears to be helpful for us to have the prospect of humiliation. Sputnik helped us fund good science - really good science: the semiconductor came out of it."

*

"Being able to see an activity log of where a kid has been going on the Internet is a good thing."

*

"I'm a great believer that any tool that enhances communication has profound effects in terms of how people can learn from each other, and how they can achieve the kind of freedoms that they're interested in."

*

"People always fear change. People feared electricity when it was invented, didn't they? People feared coal, they feared gas-powered engines... There will always be ignorance, and ignorance leads to fear. But with time, people will come to accept their silicon masters."

*

"The PC has improved the world in just about every area you can think of. Amazing developments in communications, collaboration and efficiencies. New kinds of entertainment and social media. Access to information and the ability to give a voice people who would never have been heard."

*

"In almost every job now, people use software and work with information to enable their organisation to operate more effectively."

9 PHILANTHROPY

"The Global Fund is a central player in the progress being achieved on HIV, TB and malaria. It channels resources to help countries fight these diseases. I believe in its impact because I have seen it firsthand."

*

"The Gates Foundation has learned that two questions can predict how much kids learn: 'Does your teacher use class time well?' and, 'When you're confused, does your teacher help you get straightened out?'"

*

"Although I don't have a prescription for what others should do, I know I have been very fortunate and feel a responsibility to give back to society in a very significant way."

*

"I actually thought that it would be a little confusing during the same period of your life to be in one meeting when you're trying to make money, and then go to another meeting where you're giving it away. I mean is it gonna erode your ability, you know, to make money? Are you gonna somehow get confused about what you're trying to do?"

*

"You may have heard of Black Friday and Cyber Monday. There's another day you might want to know about: Giving Tuesday. The idea is pretty straightforward. On the Tuesday after Thanksgiving, shoppers take a break from their gift-buying and donate what they can to charity."

*

"The general idea of the rich helping the poor, I think, is important."

*

"Effective philanthropy requires a lot of time and creativity - the same kind of focus and skills that building a business requires."

*

"The outpouring of support from millions of people in the immediate aftermath of the earthquake in Haiti has been impressive."

*

"The spread of online information isn't just good for charities. It's also good for donors. You can go to a site like Charity Navigator, which evaluates nonprofits on their financial health as well as the amount of information they share about their work."

*

"I remember thinking quite logically that I didn't want to spoil my children with wealth and so that I would create a foundation, but not knowing exactly what it would focus on."

*

"The most amazing philanthropists are people who are actually making a significant sacrifice."

10 PHILOSOPHY

"Just in terms of allocation of time resources, religion is not very efficient. There's a lot more I could be doing on a Sunday morning."

*

"The Internet is becoming the town square for the global village of tomorrow."

*

"I agree with people like Richard Dawkins that mankind felt the need for creation myths. Before we really began to understand disease and the weather and things like that, we sought false explanations for them. Now science has filled in some of the realm - not all - that religion used to fill."

*

"I believe that if you show people the problems and you show them the solutions they will be moved to act."

*

"The only definition by which America's best days are behind it is on a purely relative basis."

*

"I don't think culture is something you can describe."

*

"By improving health, empowering women, population growth comes down."

*

"I don't think there's anything unique about human intelligence."

*

"Expectations are a form of first-class truth: If people believe it, it's true."

*

"You can't have a rigid view that all new taxes are evil."

*

"I have been struck again and again by how important measurement is to improving the human condition."

*

"Being flooded with information doesn't mean we have the right information or that we're in touch with the right people."

*

"In almost every area of human endeavor, the practice improves over time. That hasn't been the case for teaching."

*

"I think it makes sense to believe in God, but exactly what decision in your life you make differently because of it, I don't know."

*

"Exposure from a young age to the realities of the world is a super-big thing."

*

"We all need people who will give us feedback. That's how we improve."

*

"If your culture doesn't like geeks, you are in real trouble."

*

"The belief that the world is getting worse, that we can't solve extreme poverty and disease, isn't just mistaken. It is harmful."

*

"We make the future sustainable when we invest in the poor, not when we insist on their suffering."

*

"We always overestimate the change that will occur in the next two years and underestimate the change that will occur in the next ten. Don't let yourself be lulled into inaction."

*

"Discrimination has a lot of layers that make it tough for minorities to get a leg up."

*

"I don't think there is any philosophy that suggests having polio is a good thing."

*

"If you can't make it good, at least make it look good."

*

"We've got to put a lot of money into changing behavior."

*

"Treatment without prevention is simply unsustainable."

*

"Research shows that there is only half as much variation in student achievement between schools as there is among classrooms in the same school. If you want your child to get the best education possible, it is actually more important to get him assigned to a great teacher than to a great school."

Made in the USA
Monee, IL
06 December 2019